DARK

DISCOVER ALL RADIATIONG KEYHOLES

MASRAT SHAHANA

Contents

About The Author

Masrat Shahana, a 22 years old girl who had a dream of being an author at the age of 10.Many circumstances put me down many a times but my friends always encouraged me to write. I was overwhelmed when one of my Poetries was read by my classmates Amtul Aziz, Nusrat and Afra on the occasion of children's day which completely amazed my professor. She was delighted to read my write up and asked me to continue my passion. The day when my father expired I took an oath that Mr. and Mrs Mashaq will be really proud of me. I constantly kept on working on my poetry. I even started working as an English teacher which further fuelled my spirit towards poetry. I was been awarded in literature, after which my principal Dr. Tanveer Jamal from THE CITY ACADEMY school where I was working as an teacher honoured and felicitated me for the award. I was even encouraged by my best colleagues Ms. Shagufta Jabeen , Mrs. Azra and my siblings!

About The Book

Good people and good books are not understood immediately, they have to be studied to understand. Here's a book where you get every bitter and good tastes of life. Might be you can relate it with your situations as well.

ONE

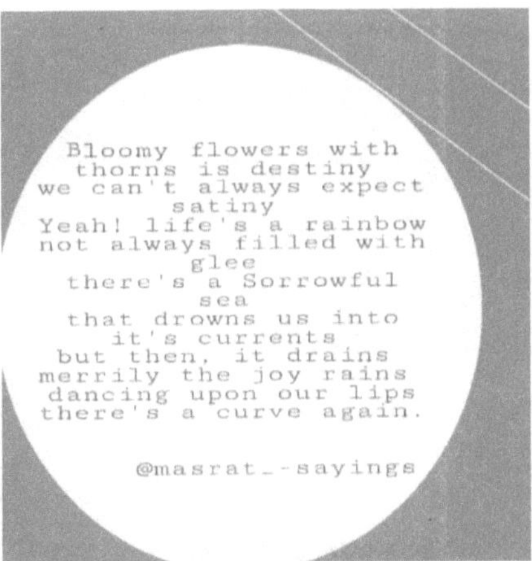

Bloomy flowers with
thorns is destiny
we can't always expect
satiny
Yeah! life's a rainbow
not always filled with
glee
there's a Sorrowful
sea
that drowns us into
it's currents
but then, it drains
merrily the joy rains
dancing upon our lips
there's a curve again.

@masrat_-sayings

TWO

❤

<pre>
          I was those
    shattered pieces of
         a s h e s
      for which to burn
      //no match stick
         was needed
       just a spark of
     heartache, could
        burn me down
         completely
    I for myself shall
   water it profoundly
    //led that fire to
       e x h a u s t
      I'll plant a weed
        of self love
       within my heart
      radiate sun rays
         towards it
    let it rise to the
          tallness
     for which one day
      the leaves of it
      could outline my
            heart
        and no such
   ignition could burn
         me again

      //masrat_sayings
</pre>

THREE

❦

Read my eyes, you'll find oceans in it
they aren't meant for you to drown
collide with those waves,
bless your soul with the aqua of my eyes

Unfold my heart
visualise the rainbow inside
strongly crave for its colours

ride through my brain
pass through the galaxies in it
and search your spark

/masrat_sayings

FOUR

My wings are not meant to be tied
And kept for ornamentation
if they are willing to make me fly firmly
they will make me glide very high
being and alluring damsel is not my
dream
a Charming soul is the actual stream
oh damn! again a tan are not my
worries
delight in the dazzling sun is my kind
of Glee
@masrat_sayings

FIVE

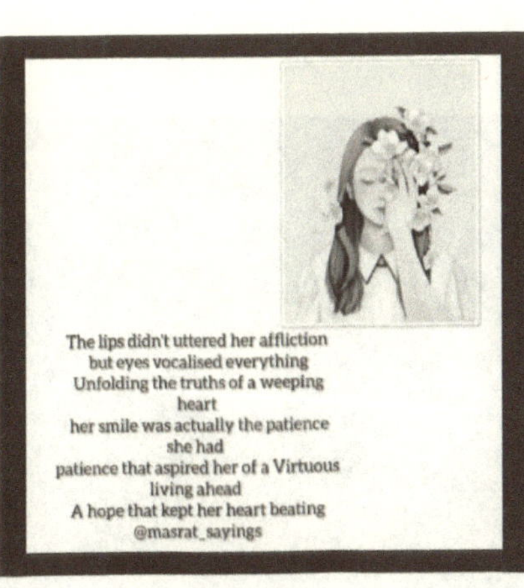

The lips didn't uttered her affliction
but eyes vocalised everything
Unfolding the truths of a weeping
heart
her smile was actually the patience
she had
patience that aspired her of a Virtuous
living ahead
A hope that kept her heart beating
@masrat_sayings

SIX

Give me a pocket of stars from the
Galaxy you have
Let me feel the feel of being a hope
When everything around is dark

@masrat_sayings

SEVEN

she is a Choco brown
yet she isn't ashamed of
writing a fairy tale
cauz she was taught
she had a heart made
of all milky whites!

EIGHT

the moment when I mastered myself
over my anxiety ,,
I begun to enjoy the alluring
atmosphere,
disregarding the dim view of my
intellectuality,,
 created by the souls who always
disliked the brightness of my smile ,
now relishing every bit of my Life by
entiting empathy to my own wit!!
                @masrat_sayings

NINE

@masrat_sayings

TEN

every night questions me where have I
lost that pocket of stars
that once shined brightly in my life..

that dark sky and my dull eye searches
for the dazzling moon

but what we get is the dark blotchy
moon

yet we smile for our togetherness..
that doesn't have any end

@masrat_sayings

ELEVEN

Thousand miles apart
I found a falling spark ,
loosing it's radiancy
I tried to reach it
to search reason for the fall
But during the journey
I was blessed with more sparkling
sparkles.....!!!

TWELVE

your tear is Pearl that is always precious
but not rare..but who are you to lessen its
cherish!
No doubt Pearl is surrounded with Majesty
..but the tear you shed is actually
breathtaking for the mortals around you..
who dwindles the value of it
let your tear be a mystery that's never
going to solved!!

@masrat_savings

THIRTEEN

A traumatic voice is always heard
uttered from my afflicted heart.
oh eyes! beware to sight the entity that isn't yours.
Voice that stops my fantasy of being a majesty, but !
This voice isn't that booming to manifest my constraints.
owing to the fact, my nightmare is the loudest of all voices
/masrat_sayings.

FOURTEEN

If I would paint my heart out
You would wonder for the
Beauty it has...
It would make you forget the
Shiny stars...
You would wonder for the shine
My heart has
It would make you forget the
Bloomy flowers
You would wonder for the prettiness
It has..
@masrat_sayings

FIFTEEN

The road was adorned with Thorns,
awarding me the misery for being
devoted to the worldly- wise mankind
was this the only present I deserve for
being a glorified soul????
the thorns prickling my underfeet
brimfilled with the red vital fluid,,
teaching me not to be too devoted,,
because not everyone deserves
goodness of a glorified soul!!
@masrat_sayings

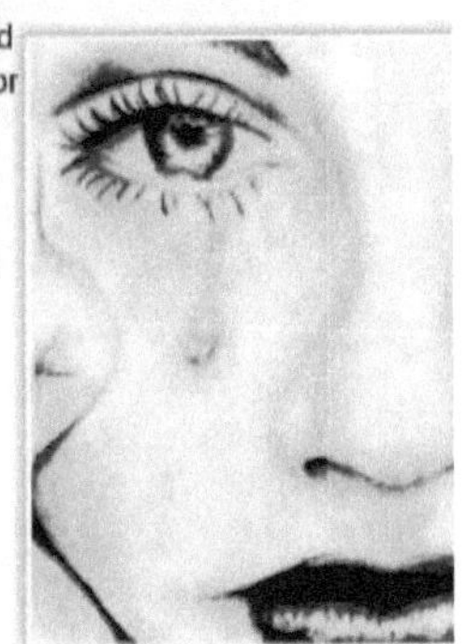

SIXTEEN

Her life is filled with different colours of pain
The pain that decreases the intensity of her laugh
But a little smile on her face
colours the rainbow of her lifell
@masrat_sayings